The Pursuit of Happiness

Also by Laurie Duggan

Poetry

East: Poems 1970–74 (1976)
Under the Weather (1978)
Adventures in Paradise (1982, 1991)
The Great Divide, Poems 1973–83 (1985)
The Ash Range (1987; 2nd edition, 2005)
The Epigrams of Martial (1989)
Blue Notes (1990)
The Home Paddock (1991)
Memorials (1996)
New and Selected Poems, 1971–1993 (1996)
Mangroves (2003)
Compared to What: Selected Poems 1971–2003 (2005)
The Passenger (2006)
Crab & Winkle (2009)
The Epigrams of Martial (2010)
Allotments (2011)

Cultural history

Ghost Nation (2001)

Laurie Duggan

The Pursuit of
Happiness

Shearsman Books

First published in the United Kingdom in 2012 by
Shearsman Books
50 Westons Hill Drive
Emersons Green
Bristol
BS16 7DF

Shearsman Books Ltd Registered Office
30–31 St. James Place, Mangotsfield, Bristol BS16 9JB
(this address not for correspondence)

www.shearsman.com

ISBN 978-1-84861-222-8

Contents

1

2

1

Letter to John Forbes

lit up in a window
with a burger & glass
of African *chenin blanc*

I'm reading the later Creeley
on Charing Cross Road

you, ten years back
in limbo (Melbourne)
of which you made the best

I inhabit an England
you mightn't recognise
though you would have read
the fine print that led here

(the market *didn't* decide
in your case).

will I echo Le Douanier, who
celebrated Picasso as 'traditional',
himself as 'modern'?

maybe

this notebook's
no 'art pad',
nor is this place

(everyone behind the counter
is from Poland)

the music:
'I am a cauliflower'
misheard from the Stone Roses

opposite: BUDWEISER,
ENGLISH BREAKFAST
'OPEN',

the only art here
is civic (a 'water feature'
from the seventies)

the buses all head north
to Clapton Pond,
but I'm southbound
for The Cut, Southwark,

poetry, spotlit
on a tiny stage

Angles 1-18

1

to be sensible
of cold, the decay
of light

2 (Uplees)

a silence
on the Swale,
or near enough:
incoming tide,
bird calls

cement slabs, on which
black-faced sheep forage

the explosive factory
blew up in 1916

3 (London Victoria)

the shake-spe-herians
rant at a neighbour table

(as the deaf would drink
at the Forest Lodge, their signs

speedy, erratic)

(poetry is not
endless speech)

the roaring queens roar on

we in the pits
put up with it

then head out for Kent

4

on Clapham High Street:
– VOLTAIRE –
– drycleaners of distinction –

5   (Brighton)

the Sunday market:
battered legs of a shop dummy
fireplaces
a broken exercise machine
Cliff Richard's 'Hits'

6

ice expected
the night of the launching

long shadows across fields
a hint of mist

sunset, south of Rochester
a sickle moon over Westminster

7

the door knob
cold to touch

frost on the western rooftops

ethereal blue plastic
on rows of vegetables

8

past the shortest day
at last

arthritis
apparently

the writing, shaky
the fog

(at least)
lifted

9

I'm not allowed to be ill
I oughtn't be, shouldn't be

lying on my back in late sun
it's chill outside, then dark

take meat out of the refrigerator
chop the Chinese cabbage

(movement of leafless vines on a neighbour wall
a rusted blue ventilator

the head of Gautama
transported into the yard
stone among the shoots

an old filing cabinet
moved to the garage

10

hop poles recede in fog
'a delay in services
due to a fatality
in the Meopham area'

11

hail over Ferry Marsh
mud underfoot at Halstead
fields of chipped crockery and stoneware

12   (Chanctonbury Ring)

after the Great Storm a broken crown
wild anemonies under the lip of the hill

13

At night

all things sleep
save rats

in the walls
(wondering if

they're any good
or not)

outside, yellow
streetlight on gillyflowers

a moss rooftop,
who knows what con-

stellation overhead
or the whereabouts

of ducks at 3am

14

a sky
full of

small
movements

15 (May again)

creeper on a wall
turns ochre green

a young blackbird
becomes
a black
bird

16 (Imagined America)

Confederates take over the village square
guitar, snare, voice and double-bass
twang, reverb & hiccup from the pub

17

a large chick balances
on the edge of a bucket

18

late light
hits the bar window

Written in a Kentish Pub on Hearing of the Death of Jonathan Williams

a
generous man

a modern
epicure

gone from
our midst

(I could knock
together something

like gammon &
mushrooms

(here, the schoolteachers
figure pints will

write reports.
another Bishop's finger?

yes, and
in memoriam.

for J.W.,
what?

photos of
Kent's finest?

(this Thatcherite
province, its

councils
comprised of

Tory
stayputs

the idiots
of small business?

(blue bins
appear

then dis-
appear

the populace
have no-

where to
put them

plastic bags
resume).

what's for
Jonathan here

the gastro-pub?
(fine unless

you contract it
(gastro)

a walk, coast
to coast

drive, for coffee
fuel

('O'NAN's
AUTO SERVICE'?

it's a world
of open

parentheses
a world

minus J.W.
'You can tell

white trash, but
you can't

tell it much
. . .'

(or you could
give it

the Bishop's
finger?

a man
in absurd

green hat
represents

St Patrick's Day
(when is it?)

now, here?
nowhere?

or a joke
(I don't know

as I don't
so many items

of customary
ritual

(no hot-cross-
buns

in this town,
Monday,

the bakery
closed.

tonight, here
in the pup

(the 'pup' . . .
no, the pub

(in the Sun
where I sing

escaping
plumbing

re-
sponsibilities, re-

views, a Yeats
biography

the drummer
from Caravan, again?

(the sadness,
progressive rock

in the provinces
in, on

or about
the premises

incognito no less
(a glow

of light
behind glass

over the bar:
pump

& circumstance,
a trail (trial?)

of spilt beer
(spilt images?)

lachrimae
rerum

& death
(over all)

jamon?
gammon?

(on the Ham
Marsh?

J.W.
R.I.P.

Grenadines

to arrive at a place
without baggage

to leave with
spectral architecture

a barman
fluent in Scouse

labelled
'the prick from Cadiz'

a river, disappearing
under a town

*

the pomegranate
a toothed apple

as wall relief
or bollard

*

Ortiz
viewed Albaicin
as dice, rolled
down a hillside

*

Images of two monks (Carthusians?), one
pierced by a spear, the other
bullet wound in the chest or
hatchet in skull.

Who are these people?

*

sword and
cross:

the cassock
goes well with

'fruit salad'

*

Baroque is
'shock and awe'

you see the virtues
of Rococo

An Italian Lake

one side shaded
for months; the other
plentiful olives, a house
on a steep hillside.
this is 'a speechless place'
says the guide: meaning
neither incomparable
nor unspeakable;
'sightless' perhaps:
a wall of shuttered villas
owned by footballers
and movie stars

Milan

1
avoid places the guide books describe as 'bohemian'
only the northern edge of Brera begins to feel like real people
live there

2
the sparrows are smaller than English sparrows
but the pigeons and blackbirds are the same size

3
in Veronese's 'Last Supper'
everyone appears drunk

4
Medardo Rosso sculpts
like wax melts

5
Balla's 'Dog on a leash'
just about describes the Quadrilatero d'Oro

6
the Stazione Centrale is under wraps
the futurists have abandoned the city

Loony Tunes

ellipse rings
a lip ring
wrung, or
wrong

*

a dog
in a
jacket

a junket

*

alias
a lie

*

a cue
a queue

align
a line

a lane
alone

*

a noun
astounds
a stoned
hound

*

a Birk-
beck
beak

*

a bit
obit

Oxenhope Revisited

1
a dormouse in the church car park
a 'wind farm' above Haworth

2
clouds hang on the moors
rain falls on the conservatory

3
the laptop
drops out

4
boots dry on the tiles
an umbrella, furled
in the garden
(a soccer ball, a pair
of spectacles
lost on the lawn

5
dark brakes
visible for miles

frequent dead rabbits

6
how do you say 'Brontë' in Japanese?

7
the rain, it rain-
eth every day

the pen, it run-
neth out

8
Oxenhope Moor to Hebden Bridge
every track a watercourse

9
'The struggling Rill insensibly is grown
Into a Brook of loud and stately march,
Cross'd ever and anon by plank and arch . . .'

10
that just about says it

Impaludism

The general morbid state occurring in
inhabitants of marshy districts.
(*OED*, 1881)

1
all or nothing at all is
everything you are
(ask me how I knew
all I've grown accustomed to
as Gyro Gearlooose
loses the plot
(what's good for the goose
is not to forget) the where-
withal of knowledge
stands on its head
in the bathroom mirror
marking time with what it can
to sunlight,
distant radio

2
encroaching shade
or pink light
up against the trellis
a fortune lost weekly
astumble between chimneys
it takes a season to angle
eaten or half-eaten
a wardrobe away
we make our shifts
as best, as worst,
as worsted, what's left

guttering in the bowl
as morning puts the stars
wound up for today

3
'idiot light' and now
hiss of water
as the room leans
to infinity, a brow
(or prow) over the street
named what? marshes
low and distant
a catalogue of beasts
line up to be milked
and all the air quiet
as gradients fall away
the Swale invades
sensibility, a land
at best marginal

4
a black painting
passages in dark red
reflect a room back
at its beholder
somewhere a zither
a movie, substance
the sky, the sea, inert
a gas, behind all this
tangle of apostrophes
outlaws appropriate
imagery, a quiz show
for those in the know
who harvest before it ends
traces of the bends

5

go book, be
a blight in
what's around
entombed in air
your staircase stretches
towards the stars
as hope is kindling
aspiring to nought
a pitch, a kind of sale
as markets crash
a bubble, perfect
of its kind
rests in a space
above the heart

6

two thousand year old
tree in Eastling
a road to nowhere
falls off the back
of the Downs, a tunnel
once been through
takes its shape then
collapses. you do not read
these letters at peril
taking sights on flowers
that light up finally
turning mulch, a bead
on what's ahead,
a head, a light

7

enough covenants
save these cushions

it's all enacted here
in this room the
dull curtains frame
take from books
what we can, isolate
instances, white walls
thick with ideograms
only the sound booms
across streets
where poetry and the risible
exist, a draft
of departing tides

Bin ends   (Dogs, Part 6)

It says here that Tony Baker makes
'sounds across the range from
free improvisation to rustic guinguette à la
moules frites'.

Refried boogie Tony?

*

Mohair

her suit
hirsute

*

nobody ever talks of their 'wasted middle age'

*

Headers

JUDGE BURNT
IN CHARD
. . .

CAT
SHOT
BY
YOBS

*

Georg Grosz

a man with a mobile,
bent over laughing

*

disposable
chopsticks

*

poetry, once a potential cause of death,
has become 'self-help'

*

The Generation Gap

'hairbrush?'
'no: "head-rush"'

*

American Poetry Shrink-Wrap

*

Responsibilities

I want to have written the review
so that I can read the book

*

Performance 2 (for Sean Bonney)

There are those who lean forward, into it
and those who lean back, out of it

*

At Lee Harwood's

to be driven at furiously
by a yellow duck on a tricycle

*

Australiana

**MUM RESCUES MAN
SAVAGED BY
WHITE POINTER**

*

Ghost Writer

advice:
add
vice

*

the smell of new mown
pneumonia

*

The Thames Estuary

forks or
forts?

*

In Bloomsbury

'a self-congratulatory glass of something is definitely in order'

*

A note

it's around 6
and I've gone
to The Sun

*

St Pancras

Old Speckled Hen
(for old speckled men?)

*

Life & Times

the usual
at the usual

*

60

the fucking enemy
disappears

*

subtleties
subtitles

*

Language Poem

alimony
al limone

*

'the only hippopotamus in Montenegro is on the loose'

*

Winter Poem

whiteness, then
Guinness

*

these guys are the wrong people
to ask for a paper-clip

*

Epiphany

a cartoon dog
in a real window

*

puzzle dust

*

Mr [   ]urine Man

*

aphasia . . . that's
the word

*

anti-poems are what poetry is;
poems are the real fakes

*

Virginia Woolf (on the wall)
wouldn't enter a place like this

*

Estuary Haiku

a Lamborghini
in East Tilbury

*

The English People Pay Homage To Damien Hirst

1) collect dogshit in plastic bags

2) hang it from trees

*

animal
vegetable
minimal

*

A salute to the Cambridge Marxists

If you're not at the High Table
you're not in the room

Oñati Notebook

For one moment only, sunlight
across the Plaza Sta Marina,

intermittent heavy rain & thunder,
dim light from low windows.

Concrete circles around trees collect the downpour,
dead leaves stick to the pavement.

I read poems by Elsa Cross, Mexican,
in English by various hands;

the mountains, even the streets,
inaccessible for now

*

Coats dance on the coat rack;
noises off from a billiard room

a rip in the table's baize,
a warp towards one pocket.

'Poetry
is all you need to do'
says Pam

and, I guess,
'it's my job'

Euskadian rhythms,
pinxto:

the mysteries
of 2009

*

Up there somewhere
are farmhouses, tiles held down by rocks,
stone paths across fields,

further, the peaks

*

A torrent erodes banks, the grassy edges
under the bridge.

Everything smells of cigarettes

Umbrellas unfurl
on the road to the monastery,
pedestrians hesitate, then run.

A ridge divides the ways to Zumarraga and Arantzazu.

*

Why is it that you only watch nature programs
if you're bored? Small beasts eaten
by larger beasts (economics?).

A few tracks improve things:
Jackie Mittoo for instance
(Kingston's Booker T),

(outside, the pavement
still shines, white arrows on a wet road,
too early for *raciones*),

the Atlantics (like the Shadows on speed),

the Throwing Muses, 'I slip . . .' – a descending scale
arrested midway (heartbreak).

My hands, the hands of a very old person,
rest on the arms of an ergonomic chair
(of Bauhaus design: Marcel Breuer?).

All this takes me away from what's out there:
a black square (homage to Ad Reinhardt)
inflected by pointillisme

*

The weather lifts,
or not,

sheep up hillsides
possibly dry tomorrow

zuria
beltza
gorria
horia
berdea
urdina
these are the Basque colours
(white, black, red, yellow, green, blue)

bat
bi
hiru
lau
bost
these, the numbers (1-5)

I have mailed my friends (a strange contraction)

and I have already forgotten who's who
in Wilkie Collins, eighty pages in

*

Answer to Philip Whalen's 'Mysteries of 1961':
'Mr Knibx' was Basque!

*

Outside the door, the sound
of a mop, inside
the click of a washing machine.

Am I light headed?
or washed-up?

'nothing in *that* drawer'

I ran out of town, meaning
there was no town left

*

Autumn trees, burnt patches amid pine

up a few steps, a peak,
unseen elsewhere, suddenly there.

Trail signs peter out or don't exist.

Back in the town hall square
observe pigeons, a barn
on the slope of that hill
(the mountains so close, so distant)

*

The mind floats
beyond all this,

                              poetries
of a past
coagulate

trapped in one language
reading becomes difficult

a drift of grammars
assonantal or consonantal shifts

the woods
above the town,

above the trees,
what fades

and what assumes a smoky light

*

Out from Oñati
on the slopes, *frutas kiwi,*
champinones y boletas

I've yet to name that sharp mountain,
its contours not visible on a map

*

San Sebastiãn / Donastia: an Art Noveau town mostly burnt
out by fires, mid 19th century, rebuilt post-Haussmann,
hence boulevards, mansard rooves, a river promenade; the
old town walled in by Monte Urgull, the port, two beaches
and a grand plaza. Across the bay a *funiculare* transports you
to the kitsch paradise of Monte Igueldo, a 1960s hotel with
amusement parks

in the distance Biarritz, the French coast.

Later, from Zumarraga
a crazed taxi driver takes 30K bends at twice that speed.

Later still: several glasses of wine

*

Arrows on a drying road
point to Arantzazu
a pocket in the mountains

Chillida's doors
a crypt by Nestor Basterretxeak

a parking lot

and way down, a stream, caves,
autumn patches on the rock face

over these mountains
rivers flow to a different sea

*

The backblocks of Oňati,
evening light on the valley side,

a comfortable bar on a backstreet intersection
the floor, brick and tile, brown woodwork.

on the walls: Basque feminist graffiti.

a cigarette machine
called РОТЭМКІЙ

*

The Palace at 12.30 pm
(homage to Giacometti)

maps are admonitions
(a clear sky, more or less

though Sol says change
comes rapidly in the mountains

*

An image of red tree roots, an installation in Trafalgar Square,
back page of the local.

Gasteiz 17°   Iruněa 18°

Bihar (tomorrow?) fine. These
the limits of understanding

OŇATIKO KARNIBALAK 2010

dancing figures of
four red peppers, an exhibition.

On the main square it's quiet
save 'a groovy kind of love' in Spanish

*

From a gap down to the river, across a tributary
then back again by footbridge

an ancient oven in the undergrowth

stone on the path marbled
like the tower of the parish church (S. Miguel)

songsters, possibly blackbirds
(too late for the *rossignol*)

The trail leads round the back of a hill (Sanbartolomegaňa)
along Arantzazu *Erreka* (Creek?), through Mutueta
over a rise back to Oňati

a redbreast
an orange-bellied slug

fog halfway up the valley

Each of these mountains
has a name,
perhaps a character

*

The four comparatives of Basque:
big
bigger
biggest
too big

a handy language in the border country through the war
(so too the now extinct language whistled in the Pyrenees,
capable of whole sentences, entire discourses)

'our words are our world . . .
what they lead us to is all we have' (Creeley)

*

At Mutueta the Arantzazu no longer drops to a pool
(as it did this morning), backing up instead
against the stone wall

*

On the square, two men drink wine and beer for breakfast,
a mirror pretends further information,
the space 'behind' different from this one.

A cigarette smoulders at an empty table
a smoking *mesa.*

The wall in here features an old black & white photograph
of THE MOUNTAIN, no credit, no information

I'll head that way I think,
but, no, I won't, I'm going south.

When I turn around
it's there, like Fuji

*

Everyone heads here (the café
with no name), 10.00 am.
Am I going anywhere?
Others seem about to, but don't

I always make the mistake
that other people have destinations
like that man in the T-shirt:
'Fiesta, yes! And I'd like a beer too!'

A small grey bird (smaller than a sparrow)
black & white head and tail feathers
skims the river that flows under the church

*

Is it? could it be (the peak)?
Landurratzko Punta,
with Klabeliñaitz (or Marizelaieta)
a little to the left?

the contours are about right

it would *have* to be
unpronounceable

right on the border of this province/region

Oňatiko

Paphos

Darkness across the water, before which
lightning, hail against windows;
a morning of tombs and low scrub, the desire
to get 'shit-faced' in some bar

The term 'authenticity' is meaningless here,
even the ruins attest to constant change

Sea-horse duct above rooftop generators,
satellite dishes, air-conditioning units, hot water services
VISIT PAPHOS AQUARIUM and
CHRIS HOLIDAY RENT A CAR
An illuminated truck circles the town
playing Christmas carols
Santa Claus awash on the seafront

At night a manhole cover, lifted by waves
clanks in the middle distance;
the sea flattens out
with a slight breeze from Africa

The cats of Paphos exist as small clues
in a big picture

A bar that sports mixed drinks:
'sex on the beach' and 'blow job'
hosts a band that plays 'Down Under'

The old is new, the new is old,
nea and *kato*
('an after dinner sleep
dreaming of both')

Everything here is 'English'd
by various hands'

insomnia?
That's a Greek word

Little Journal

1

From last century, the art
of Henri Laurens: its domestic scale
alive in our moment of ones and zeros

2

Once, in the 5ième, on Avenue Gay-Lussac,
I stayed in a triangular apartment,
balcony adjoining the bathroom,
travelled north through Place Monge,
named for a geometer, its stalls
of onion and garlic, en route
for the International City of Art

3

Metal chimney extensions ascend
a wall by a viaduct, seeking light;
the park below inhabited by empty bottles

4 (July 14)

After a washed out parade
an image of the General
commands blank space
before the Hôtel de Ville

Après midi, the clouds scatter,
commandos drop into the Tuileries
protected by gendarmes
as they fold their chutes

Angles 19-32

19 (St Ives)

pink balls of thrift
cling to the rocks

20

rain on a Kentish garden,
an overflowing pond,
the rusted cone of a green ventilator,
then the sky clears, partly

21

snow scraped to the side of Uplees road
a lost motorist heads for the Shipwright:
nothing out here but concrete blocks in fields

22

nail holes, woodworm . . .
the beam's still solid

23

down the shade end of the yard
soil hangs like rock from grass roots

24

a pheasant ate the jasmine leaves

25

antirinnhums,
box of six, kitchen end
of the yard, before
the dwarf rose,
iris about to bloom,
monkshood, michaelmas
daisies settling in

26 (Estuary)

sulphurous airs
through Rainham, Essex,

then, south of the river
the waste of Ebbsfleet,

a car park surrounds the station

27

beyond the shipyard the town ends:
a plank bridge over a tidal channel
then Nagden Marsh, the Swale,
the tip of Sheppey; at night
Southend lit across the estuary

28

left bank of the Creek
a dyke edges Ham Marsh
to the junction with the Oare,
the white timber Shipwright

29

a string of houses, south
on the Ashford road and the A2;
beyond, a field of buttercups, a
collapsed barn

30

the irregularity of bricks
smoke blackened,
patches of limewash,
a pale fossil at the foot of a staunchion

31

red-tailed kites
over ploughed fields, Bucks.

32

a realist painting:
the chip eaters

The Exeter Book

or, as Lee had it
                        a hand
from a cloud, grasp-
ing
a pint?

sooty gulls preen
on the Exe,
geese
                    ('you wouldn't want
                    one of those flying into you'
                    the impaired man

he's absolutely right

those hills beyond the A377
down the bottom of the street

a wind, almost
Atlantic

in a bar with
the Unofficial Roy Fisher
                            opposite
Gibson's Plaice
(fishmongers)
                        above it (improbably)
an Australian flag

DOVER SOLE
SCALLOPS   BRILL
DABS   TURBOT
WILD TROUT

Topsham, the bridge
over the muddy Exe,
Dutch gables,
'Georgia on my mind'

upstairs, in the quiet
of The Ship, windows
view a wall, a
ventilator calligram:

Ο Ο Ο Ο Ο Ο
∩ ∩ ∩ ∩ ∩ ∩

white paint
obscures the rest

the back of a man, sculpted
on a chair, a mansard,
hedges in distant fields

the rumble below
of Exeter Central

sun beats down on the fenced off
Royal Albert Memorial Museum

in 2011: 'all will be revealed'

The London Road

1

rough joins where beams from ships
slot into the neighbour walls;

intrusions of ironmongery
behind the curtains

the sun at an angle
manages the northern window

half-illumined furniture trapped
by slight twists, each wall a false perspective

striations in an enormous fireplace

a dark house intersected by light

2

a
cloud
moves
over
a
yellow
field

drips hang on the underbase of a bird bath

3

at the edge of town a car yard and an archaeological excavation
toward Londinium, on Watling Street
over the hill, Stone Chapel, the dry valley of Syndale

stinging nettle, dead nettle, dock, cow parsley, goose grass
    (near North Street)

forget-me-not, buttercup, stitchwort
    (near Plumford)

westward,
hands pull rope around a sheaf of
what?
wheat? asparagus?
Lamb's Conduit
FOUNDED 1843

old hinges of a former door
painted over

2

the nathan papers

1

eucalyptus after rain, even this, trunks straight or sinuous, reminds of Sydney Long. art has made this environment, its pathways, marked, curve toward the dormitories

*

red mahogany (not 'real' mahogany, just a variety of eucalypt). and in the low-lying areas stringybark and needlebark. the path goes up the ridge. underbrush. a side track revegetating

*

forest on a hill
small brush turkey with undeveloped tail
furiously running

the science of this?　　　mound building?

*

I never *wanted* to be a poet. not like some people want to be one now. it just happened. and then it was too late to do otherwise

*

the template is buried (or burned), the elsewhere to this *this* for which I function (among others) as an *as if*. 'imagine that all these things you've been taught are meaningless'. or slide into pure consumerism

*

iridescent bird shapes to scare birds off.
bolted shadecloth. fresh wind from the south

*

what if it were all like *dejeuner sur l'herbe*, those figures middle
distance of cardboard, people passing in and out of substantiality?

*

my hands are foxed

*

we hear so many accents (at the Capital they hear only their
own). in consequence, we are never sure of the sound of poems
from elsewhere. this translates into an instability of our own
soundings. if the sound of what we read as poetry bears not
much relation to the original intent we may be less aware of
poetry's musical dimension

*

on the edge of sleep. black spiral binding, blue check bedspread

*

the great cake sails down the river

*

how approximate is this art?

*

an orange flies through the air en route to the dorms

*

'you need a mess of help to stand alone'

*

rain in the atmosphere. the dampness of paper

*

driving to the Gold coast, the theme from 'Get Carter',
and back in the rain Mitch Mitchell's cymbals hiss
on a barely visible road

*

poetry – the opposite of political speech? (that makes you think
you *can* understand it)

*

crimson on the balcony against a yellow wash. a thunderous sky
dims to bronze and cobalt, then pink and grey, then monochrome

the lit ferries and streetlights

David Roback's effects pedal forces sustain into overtone

*

psychedelic verities

*

the rail track of mild techno. a music that says we are busy, we
have things to do

*

small scented bushes fringe the cafeteria

*

Sky News: 'alleged yob speaks',
a panda walks on hind legs,
Saddam in underpants, Kylie's breast ok

*

Mike Parr's drawing. his painterly aspects
Ian Burn's 'value-added' landscapes.

*

no matter how smart you are you can still be floored by Taj
Mahal (with the Rising Sons) singing '2.10 Train'

2

cnr Kent & Liverpool Sts, breakfast
Chinese English, its charm
'Mellow Real Estate'
'Eating World'

*

I thought 'maybe this is too long', but then I thought 'it's too
late to stop now'

*

children going mad in the camps

*

dogshit bag

a woman with very long legs, as though on stilts, her trousers
too short.

smoke hovering behind those on their way to work

is the 'city' of 'poetry' a 'city of poetry'?

*

Wynyard bus station, 5.15pm. alcohol made waiting so much
easier. 'something to do with your hands' (but so is this writing,
if perhaps less discreet). opposite the Occidental, the limited
stop buses to Avalon and points north. York St, 63-43, the AWA
building, deco and 60s facades

*

lost places:

the Green Iguana (Newtown)
the Prince Edward Hotel (Darlington)
Nicholas Pounder Bookseller (Double Bay)
but not Nicholas Pounder

*

the moon through haze, 6am

'where armed men
can behave abominably
without fear of punishment' (Amnesty report)

*

sunlight (the park) at the end of the street

MARTIN LUTHER KIRCHE   AD 1881

*

a doughnut at an angle looks like a black pudding

*

the pop movie/video trope of the group running into shot

the contrast between how bands appear adult in the video and young in the interview. is this the difference between self-image and outsider perception?

*

Coltrane's great 1950s title: 'midriff'

*

at the MoS café. winter air and daylight through the columns.
the harbour evidenced by visible sky between buildings

rush hour (Grace Cossington Smith)

'real' coffee

*

even in this city a distant train siren

superscript

no radio

upstairs from Charlie Chan's Pool Hall (currently under
renovation), an arcade that funnels and veers left, of clothes, dry
cleaners, Chinese snack food

the bare grey of these streets, 8.15 Saturday morning
the part-stumble, part walk of small children and robots

3

a question mark inside a pair of inverted commas

*

4pm parrots
raucous in gutterings
the sky over dark buildings
driving, visor down
to the city

*

the idea of singing a landscape. relate this to the old projectivist talk of 'breathing'. but here the unit has more to do with what is 'expressed' than with lung capacity

*

container vessel

*

brown needles of sheoak.
a brush turkey, perilous on upper branches

*

if it were a kind of dance, a kind of comedic ballet, it would mean knowing where parts of the body might land, on what rock or promontory, and to which horizon the gestures are made

*

a minute red insect crosses the table between wood flecks and is
blown away

*

it's hard for me to conceive how these trees were viewed as 'drab'.
subtle rather. how would I manage otherwise?

rain through shadow tents. the girth of those birds. grasping
claws, a slippery pavement devoid of sustenance

grey maintenance building through the trees

. . . in which nothing happens

*

anthropologist among the carriers of prospecti, the futures of
institution. the wash-up of examinations. unwatched daytime
TV. imagine the camera, the casing &c, the blue downlights,
fans no longer circulating. a row of bottles, one large one in a
wooden case. doors that slide to screen a room. a room in a room

*

eaves dripping in grey light, wet tables out on the concrete.

a bird, smaller than a magpie, darkish long beak, black head,
white breast, fawn (or grey) back and wings, a prominent
gurgling call

4

the glare edging into summer. underbrush. what are the genes
of words and what structures are we condemned to repeat? the
machines write poetry, the poets build machines—or think they
do. but the machines are smarter than the poets.

a certain redundancy.

*

Noosa, or Style over Substance. though I don't mind.
at least the shop music is better.

maybe not.

a man runs with a block of ice.

we will be leaving all of this behind.

green sail, white sand, blue sky.

mountains up north. this is the Coral Sea.

lawn meets native grass.

Sheoaks – trees that give no shade.
Moreton Bay Figs – trees that do.

a peninsula (the Head), rainforest in the dips.

*

the notebook as a record of failure. I mean in the sense that only
a few words of innumerable pages make it in any interesting way.
not these.

what happened to the young man in that photograph? Petersham 1972.

the main problem for older writers must be boredom. But boredom can also produce writing . . . though not if you're bored by the writing . . .

*

the words 'bored' and 'writing' overheard from an adjacent table.

*

storms that skirt the city

people are turning into product. their organized (for them) soundtracks. products that buy other products. capitalism would prefer a world of replicants.

the slight azure.

backdated milk in the common room.

the kookaburras are sated. and the shining owls have no effect.

*

Discussing poetry with W_____. His justification for writing it is—in a sense—that it's not poetry. But he still wants it to be valued as if it were. If it doesn't work in English he will say 'but it's not written in English'.

*

the differing textures of all these trunks. the strands and components of a world.

*

x & y, the pier
a screen of fish, a moon
over those washed-up planks
colour in a late sky
escapes edges of the paper

*

a tropic world
of night illuminations
as air is water
a searchlight swept through cloud
the landscape below revealed by lightning

*

misread: tall boy
for toy ball

there is too much philosophy

the language stumbles

*

already it's summer. slight deformity of a crushed toe (impossible
to 'point' on, but I never wanted to be a dancer).

*

my Florentine notebook

*

'The sensation of needing to construct one's relation to the foreign reality is one of the problems and pleasures of tourism.'
—Robert Harbison

(what have I learned on the weekend? the 'Oxford comma', before 'or' and 'and')

a crowd panicked by difference
no better than its perceived enemies.

5

at 9am they ask 'how has your day been?'

*

on belief in poetry as 'observation', the increasing prominence
of 'reality' TV, the breakdown of distinctions between fiction
and documentary

*

tea & rain

lifting floor
lifting paint

grey out to the airport
where's the 'music' in this?

syllabub

the digits move on

*

the 'brooding Anzac'. what else?

*

Caesar's a lad!
Caesar salad

*

autocannibalism

*

'I can't go on / I go on'

*

the voices on all those tapes. missing persons. except the
persons, for the most part, are me

*

letters to various people

*

omission of margins. the wanted small detail.

iconic breakfast. look closely enough and everything changes.
the imagists were wrong, perhaps. movie music.

maybe poetry should be like a girl's scrapbook circa 1960?
horses,
horses,
horses . . .

*

almost since I started this notebook I have had 'nothing to
write'

and I am writing it

6

a slight stain on the binding, possibly sun-screen.

*

In the 19th century art became too self-important and we have to rescue ourselves from this. It's why there is always massive resentment towards it. Yes, there's money involved, but it's never really enough to warrant the detractors' ire. It's not the money so much as the rhetoric surrounding art's administration that causes the heat to rise. Even without money the early 20th century 'shock of the new' came out of a sense that it was important for the public to comprehend art. So a 'horse' that didn't 'look like a horse' was cause for complaint. When the avant-garde became respectable enough to be funded by governments there was still a sense that the artists had social duties over and above their practices; even if (in the visual arts) those duties were mainly 'value added' ones. It became ok then to be 'incomprehensible' so long as you had market skills. But all this leaves an art that plays with its own fragility without much in the way of understanding or support.

*

'I didn't sleep at all last night' (Bobby Lewis)

*

dead wood cut down
odour of underbrush

designs on sleeves appear as tattoos

*

the whole thing unravels from the edges

*

The 'I' is a function. It's the locus (almost wrote 'locust') of what purports to happen. you could discover through research what kind of sandwiches I eat (BLT today) but would it change your reading? If I were asked whether poetry was 'fiction' or 'non-fiction' I'd answer 'neither'.

*

Songs that don't end; they just stop. Is this faith in invention? Or its opposite?

*

Our letters crossing in space. Civilization and its discontents.

*

It's nearly 2pm Eastern Standard Time as I write this. Brisbane resuming its subtropical regime. Downpours at intervals (like ones I remember being drenched by, aged 16, when the trams were battleship grey—and still existed).

*

fake wood grain
the eyes of an owl

*

fretless music

7

dawn
amber lights of Hataitai

pissing into the landscape

*

I am fifty-six years old
  (almost fifty-seven)
what have I done to deserve this?

*

the rumble of small aircraft. a semicircle of sky, mountains
lower right, a flagpole left. cloud at medium altitude.

thorns squeak against the window. the sun disappears behind
Mt Victoria.

*

rain   (I don't mind)
thin cloud   selecting the landscape
light boxes hang on the slopes
                                        quake country

gradations
the tall windows
a rainbow down the valley

fog
out over the airport

*

that every other country's money looks like play money reveals
that all money is really just play money. it's only ourselves who
are deceived.

*

a day in the Gallery where no-one is allowed to wear black

*

squally

everything cold and slightly damp to the touch
(my wallet)

on the sill little cups with Malevitch designs

(waipapa hum mow mow)

still the odd light up the rise, 9.30 am

*

characteristic square gables
large rectangles of glass

rain as steam
crossing rooftops

sundecks for
what sun?

*

black shoes, black jeans, black shirt, black jumper,
red socks

*

invisible hills

*

south wind up the steps from the University
the museum full of outmoded toys, dated technology

*

the grey curtain parts
a baroque sky appears

*

amber lights
no stars yet
refractions from
raindrops
the scraping of
a rose bush
a hemisphere
of panes
black space
a tree in the yard
books in various piles

The Winds of Wellington   (a documentary)

*

high pitched birds
trees bent double

a strange blueness

*

cloud surf round Taranaki

the west coast   blue metal
basalt edge   black current

gradual removal of clothing between Wellington & Brisbane

this landscape needs to be seen in panels

a cheap bottle of gin
an ocean of small sadnesses

*

In the departure lounge:
'Are you flying?'

'I'm not catching a bus'
(they don't get it)

mud banks

peaks that shelve off to the sea
at Piha Beach

(an endless circular conversation:
'yiss . . . yiss . . . yiss')

'expect delays'

8

the flightpath image on screen, with Chinese characters, of the
Channel, Flanders and Kent

*

title for an English book: Pebbledash

*

Cambridge: the ferry path Nick Drake walked down!

*

outlandish goose pimples or
a pink pile jumper

Bonjour M'seu Barrett! (the Original Syd)

*

installed in Dr Power's rooms I think of colour schemes
honking geese and pink blossoms

'a host' &c

jonquils too
and blue daisies (?)

*

even on a relatively grey day the light in Kettle's Yard is
warm and diffuse

gathered stones. the surrealism of roots, of nature made strange
(or revealed so)

the very idea of a 'collection'
that one thing next to another could itself seem 'natural'

*

try not to spread things out too much in these rooms
or they may never find the suitcase again

*

a tripping bird
(mincing gait)

*

what do you make of a place where anyone is a possible
celebrity?

*

in a place like this it is *expected* that you take notes.

a man cuts up a newspaper . . . .
. . . .

'persons of interest' . . . .
. . . .

a well-groomed young punk: 'The Rancid Transplants' . . . .
. . . .

*

people who used to sit around writing things like this were once considered mad. I remember all of the 'writers' who would come and sit in the City of Sydney Public Library circa 1972. some had volumes full of writing. but often it was the same thing, over and over. the same sentence, the same phrase, the same word. as though there was a blockage somewhere. even a lapse of memory, meaning each sentence, each word was, for the scriptor, a completely new utterance.

maybe the band should be called Pig Latin?

*

in the dining hall, Eliot College, Kent:

spark of static from a metal chair
woodgrain on a diagonal
new books, sunglasses,
various printed matter from the banks
leather jacket
the hollow of an octagon, this hall
where I am, earthed for the moment
'please use handrail'
tinkle of a mobile
small vernacular moments
among red chairs, brickwork, bad public art
a grid of light, scaffolded above,
the sign of a running man, white on green, an arrow for direction

*

the ancient city full of tourists, language scholars, school groups
its closed promenades crowded to capacity

inscriptions of authors
trails of fame

*

a fine hair
embedded in the paper

glasses trodden underfoot

Acknowledgements

'The London Road' appeared in *An Unofficial Roy Fisher* (ed. Peter Robinson, Exeter: Shearsman, 2010) and in the limited edition *Leaving Here* (Brisbane: Light-Trap, 2012). Various poems were included in *Salamanders & Mandrake: Alan Halsey & Gavin Selerie* (Wakefield: Is Press, 2009) and *Uplift: a samizdat for Lee Harwood* (Hove, Artery Editions, 2008). Sections from 'Angles' appeared in Chinese translation in *Fires Rumoured about the City* (Macau: ASM, 2009) and two portions of 'The Nathan Papers' appeared in *For the time being: the Bootstrap book of poetic journals* (ed Tyler Doherty & Tom Morgan, Lowell: Bootstrap Press, 2007). Thanks to the editors of these publications, and thanks too to the editors of *Best Australian Poems 2009*, *Best Australian Poems 2010* (Black Inc.), *Gangway* #40, *Golden Handcuffs Review*, *Jacket2*, *Litter*, *Oban 06*, *otoliths*, *Salt* and *Southerly* in which further pieces from this book first appeared.

My special thanks to Kay Ferres, David Ellison and Griffith University for an eighteen month residence in 2005–2006. 'The Nathan Papers' was written during that residency.

www.ingramcontent.com/pod-product-compliance
Lightning Source LLC
Chambersburg PA
CBHW022202080426
42734CB00006B/541